WRITING: PLAIN & SIMPLE

George Wilhite

Texas State Technical College Waco

TSTC
Publishing

TSTC Publishing
Texas State Technical College Waco
3801 Campus Drive
Waco, TX 76705

http://publishing.tstc.edu/

Publisher: Mark Long
Editor: Kayla Allen
Project manager: Grace Arsiaga
Printing production: Bill Evridge
Interior illustrations: James Haug
Cover design: Jessica Luckey
Page layout: Stacie Buterbaugh (smbuterbaugh8@yahoo.com)
Indexing: Michelle Graye (indexing@yahoo.com)

Manufactured in the United States of America

Second edition

Table of Contents

Preface

Students testing into developmental writing classes often have a couple of overriding concerns. First, many of them feel they "can't write" or are "bad at writing" from being in other English courses. Second, this feeling is enforced because they have been taught, by every writing class since they began school, the exact same way.

Pick up any K-12 writing book and you will probably see, if you look past all the differences, a book that has 10 or 20 pages on "The Writing Process" and then commits the remainder of the book to readings and to "Methods of Rhetoric" in some way, shape, or form.

Inherent in these books is an absolute belief that a student cannot write unless he has the "vocabulary of English" so that he and the teacher can communicate. My opinion is that this makes it easier for the instructor, not the student, and that it gives instructors an "out" for when students can't learn to write. Now, that is probably overly harsh. There are a lot of good writing instructors out there who use these very same books to produce excellent writers, but if you put these books in the hands of instructors who do not understand the writing process well, students may have problems. I get those students every semester.

What I have attempted to do in this book is expand ever so slightly on those first 10-20 pages of most composition books. I want to take the VERY BASIC ideas of writing an essay and simplify them into a series of steps beginning writers can figure out on their own. I want them to use these steps until they become natural and instinctive. I want them to "internalize" the writing process.

All too often, writing books and instructors just assume that students know the writing process. That is why most books give it so little space before jumping into the much more complex information.

In this book, I focus on mainly argumentative essays (or arguing, or persuasive, or whatever the newest book decides to call it). I want to give students ONE pattern for an essay and let them get that one down before I start confusing them with other kinds of essays. Plenty of time for that in their freshman composition class. If they do, by the end of my class, understand how to put a basic essay together, then they have a foundation upon which they can build. If they understand what an introduction does, THEN they have a better chance of understanding the different ways they can introduce an essay, which they will learn in freshman composition. And so on for all the different parts of the essay. So, in this book, I will focus on, rather than skip over, the writing process.

One of the key points for instructors using this book is the makeup of the semester that I use and why. I spend an incredible amount of time during the first half of the semester going through this book unit by unit. Every one of the students works on the same prompt (college versus high school). Every one of them comes up with a thesis statement that looks incredibly like everyone else's. There's a reason for this. I want them to see WHAT needs to be in a thesis statement. We don't focus on "grabbing the reader's attention" in the introduction; we focus on the thesis statement. About the only thing most of my developmental students remember about introductions is that they should grab the reader's attention. They have no clue that it should introduce your topic, your opinion about that topic, and the reasons you have that opinion. Once they know that, they are in a much better position to produce a readable essay.

One of the things I do in the first half of the semester is try to build the students' confidence in their writing ability. I emphasize that any group of writers I address—whether developmental students, freshman composition students, senior English students, or professional fiction writers—all make the same Top 10 Mistakes (see Appendix A). One group may make them more often, but they all make the same mistakes. I have worked with fiction contests, anthologies, newspapers, magazines, and students over the last 30 years, and every one of those groups had problems with the Top 10 Mistakes. These are the ones I consider basic for any writer in any situation. There are many, many other mistakes writers can make (tone, voice, mixed metaphors, etc.), but the basic mistakes are the biggest hindrance to developmental writers. Besides the fact that many of the more advanced mistakes become increasingly subjective, those advanced mistakes are often hidden by bad grammar, bad punctuation, bad spelling, and bad organization. (Yes, I said "bad.") Let's take care of the basics first, then work on the more advanced stuff in freshman composition.

So, I spend the bulk of the first part of the semester walking students through the units of the book to produce a rough draft that they turn in somewhere close to the middle of the semester. We spend a lot of time on prewriting and "how to" prewrite. The more time they spend on this, the less time they spend on writing later because they know where they are going and get there faster. I don't "grade" their thesis or their organization plan or any of the stuff we do in the units. People learn a lot of stuff without ever being graded on it. I never got a grade on swinging a baseball bat, but I learned it.

If you feel (or your supervisor or school feels) that you absolutely have to give grades the first part of the semester, I've found that I can make all these units (and even grammar tests on the Top 10 Mistakes) quiz grades that all equal one major test grade. I could care less if the students can make 100 on each of the pieces if they cannot put it all together in the end for an essay, so my major grades come from the five or more essays the students produce in the second half of the semester.

Because there are 10 units that I cover in the first half of the semester, this is the perfect time to assign SHORT, BRIEF explanations of the Top 10 Mistakes for each unit. I might give students a brief breakdown—in plain English—of what a fragment is, the kinds of fragments there are, and ways to fix a fragment the week we're on Unit Two with a SHORT quiz at the end of that week. Then comma splices and run-ons during Unit Three. But let them know that these grades are NOT what is important. Learning to spot these mistakes and fix them is important.

I love to use Strunk & White's *Elements of Style* because it is much less intimidating than most grammar books. Of course, it doesn't have any lessons or assignments, but I like that. Rather than spending time on in-book practices, I can tailor examples to fit my students' needs. If you have a favorite grammar book, use that for the quizzes—but focus on the Top 10 Mistakes.

One of the main reasons I break the process down into ten units is so that we can spend more time on each of these units. Above all, I try to have fun with my classes. We joke about the mistakes. We roll our eyes, scream out loud, or feign fainting as we find goofs in students' papers (anonymous, of course) or on tests or quizzes. We have a hoot when coming up with a list for prewriting ("Alligator?! Who the heck has an alligator for a pet?") and other parts of the process.

I hope this book works for your developmental writing class and that you have, like I have, students that come up at the end of the semester and say, "Okay, NOW I understand what they were talking about all those years in English classes."

Introduction: Before You Write

How You Think About Writing is Important

Writing is NOT some God-given gift to a few exceptionally intelligent human beings. I know many extremely smart people who cannot write well enough to get their point across. I also know some folks who are much less "intelligent" yet have excellent writing skills. Of course, all of us have varying degrees of ability—in writing, in sports, in fashion sense. However, if you can speak the English language (and especially if you are a native English speaker), there is an excellent chance that you will be able to write effectively. Those students whose first language is one other than English often have different, more specific problems with writing that are best addressed from an English as a Second Language (ESL) perspective.

Five Basic Writing Concepts

I. Writing is a Learnable Skill

Writing CAN be learned. Many people think they can't learn to write. Often, this is because they have been told they can't write or because they have convinced themselves they can't write the same way as "good" writers in their classes. A large percentage of "non-writers" or "bad" writers don't realize how much they DO understand about writing; they just need to give themselves a chance. Many times, these writers only need to have some part of the writing process explained in a way that they understand.

II. Writing is a Process

Writing is a process, and like all processes, there are steps and techniques that can help you learn the process. As with most processes, practicing the steps and techniques in the process makes you better at the process. A batter who never learns how to hold the bat will never be able to hit well. A batter who learns how to hold the bat but doesn't practice will also never hit well.

III. The Writing Process can be Broken Down into Steps

The writing process, seen as a whole, can be terribly confusing. This is often the reason many people don't like to write. By breaking the process down into simpler, more understandable steps, you can get a better idea of what is expected at each step. It's sort of like trying to eat a sixteen-ounce steak. If you try to eat it in one big bite, you will probably choke and gag. However, if you cut that steak up into manageable bites, it is much easier to eat. With writing, if you look at a paragraph or an essay as a whole and think you can't do it, you will get stressed. One way to get rid of that stress is to see the essay (or even a paragraph) as a series of simple steps, each one by itself easy to master.

IV. Preparation & Organization Always Help

One of the main reasons many people have problems writing is that their paragraphs and essays do not seem to make sense. These writers jump around and the reader cannot understand what they are talking about. Pre-writing techniques can help them to come up with ideas and organize those ideas into an easily readable paper.

V. The Writing Process is Made up of Three Parts

The writing process can be broken down into three parts: PRE-WRITING, WRITING, and POST-WRITING. Another common mistake made by "bad" writers is that they often do only the middle part of the process. Many never do any pre-writing to help them come up with appropriate ideas and organize them, and many never do the post-writing part of the process to find mistakes in their writing and to correct them. Their papers are often unorganized and rambling, and they are full of misspelled words and common grammar mistakes.

The Three Stages of ~~Grief~~ Writing

Most people would rather attend a funeral (their own or someone else's) than write a paper. In fact, it's typical for people to spend more time agonizing over not getting started writing than doing the actual writing itself. But, that's usually because they don't feel like they have control (or even a solid understanding) of the writing process. However, by breaking the writing process into three basic stages—pre-writing, writing, and post-writing—it is possible to minimize—though not eliminate—the amount of mental anguish endured.

I. Pre-Writing

Pre-writing is the beginning phase of the writing process. Generally, you are writing in response to a prompt. Many prompts come in the form of a short paragraph of background information that ends with a question. These types of prompts are usually designed to get you thinking about a particular topic like gun control, abortion, discrimination, reality TV, citizens' rights, and so on. The object of this type of prompt is that you think seriously about what you already know about this subject and that you try to get your point across to another student or the teacher.

A second type of prompt is the essay test question: in history, for example. These questions do not usually have as much background information because they are testing your knowledge of information you have previously studied. They are often looking for specific information you have already read or discussed in class to see if you have retained that information accurately. One example would be that a history test might ask you to give three causes of the Civil War so the instructor can evaluate how well you have learned that material. You must know the information much better to answer an essay question than to answer a multiple choice question.

II. Writing

This is the part that most people think of as writing: you actually write down sentences in paragraph form to answer a question or to provide information to someone. This is often the hardest part for most people because they actually have to put their ideas down on paper in a way that others can understand. They are often scared that they will make a mistake and be made fun of. It is often the most stressful time for many writers because they can't think of ideas, they are worried about mistakes, they think they don't know anything about the subject, or any number of other reasons. This CAN BE, however, the EASIEST part of the process, as we will see later.

III. Post-Writing

Post-writing is where you check your work for mistakes and correct them, polishing your writing until it is the best it can be. This is another stage that is often overlooked by beginning writers. Proofreading and editing is another way of referring to this stage. Just a quick look at the paper is not enough; you must look hard at your work, specifically for the kinds of mistakes most commonly made. Don't worry; you will learn what to look for when we study this phase of writing.

NOTES:

Unit One: Prewriting
Part 1 - Generating Ideas

This unit will present several methods of generating ideas about a topic for a paragraph or essay.

Learning Objectives

At the end of this unit, you will:

1. be able to brainstorm for ideas;

2. be able to show those ideas in several different written forms (mapping, listing, outlining); and

3. be able to pick the best ideas to serve as major points for the essay.

General Overview

The next units—Generating Ideas, Achieving Coherence, and Persuasion—are kind of a stopping point in the process. These units will provide you with information you need to continue to "develop" or add more and better information to your main points and make the paper more understandable and more pleasant to read.

These units will help you to come up with better information for your points and put the points in an order that makes sense to the reader. All too often, readers quit reading, not because they don't understand the words, but because the words and ideas are presented in a way that is not easy to understand—out of order, with details that don't fit the topic, etc. These units, along with the process we are doing, will help with those problems.

Generating Ideas

There are many places to get ideas for your paragraph or essay. Most come from your own brain, based on information it has stored throughout your life. For example, can you think of a traumatic event that has happened to you, your family, or a friend?

Wilhite's Writing Wisdom:

What about that car wreck you or someone you know had? Or the time you were worried about the health of a family member or friend? You don't have to look elsewhere for that kind of information. It is right there in your memory, waiting to be pulled up and examined. Sometimes, you just need to give your brain a little help to find that information.

Brainstorming

Brainstorming is the exercise of writing down ideas that come to your mind about a particular topic. Like freewriting, this exercise lends itself to generating general ideas as well as generating details and examples for specific subjects.

There are several ways to help your brain generate ideas. Now we'll take a look at six of them.

I. Freewriting

Freewriting is one of the best ways to generate ideas or to cure "writer's block." When ideas won't come to you or when you are stuck at a certain point in your paper, use freewriting to get your brain searching for more information. Here's how it works:

Take several blank pieces of paper and your pen. Set a timer for between fifteen and thirty minutes (the longer, the better). As soon as you turn the timer on, start writing on the blank paper. DON'T STOP WRITING UNTIL THE TIMER GOES OFF. Even if you have to write, "I don't have anything to write" or "What is the point of this?" or "Duh," just keep writing until the timer goes off. Your brain will get tired of writing nothing and will eventually start to feed you ideas to write about. DO NOT WORRY ABOUT PUNCTUATION, SPELLING, GRAMMAR, OR ANYTHING ELSE AT THIS POINT. YOU JUST WANT TO GET SOME IDEAS DOWN ON PAPER. In the famous words of Indiana Jones's father in *Indiana Jones and the Last Crusade*: "I find that if I just sit down to think … the solution presents itself!"

Noted twentieth-century author Ernest Hemingway said, "All you have to do is write one true sentence" in regard to writer's block. That simple trick will get your brain flowing. However, some of our brains are more stubborn than others. So, it may take a thirty-minute session of freewriting for those brains to generate that one simple sentence. Often, it will not even be a sentence. Freewriting many times generates snatches of sentences—phrases, clauses, words. When you review your freewriting, though, you will probably note several words in the writing that are ideas you would like to write about or that fit with the topic you were thinking of when you started freewriting.

II. Focused Freewriting

This is the same as freewriting above, except that now you try to focus your mind on one topic. This topic may be an assigned topic from a class, one you've chosen to write on, or one that came to your attention from unfocused freewriting.

III. Listing

One of the most common methods of generating ideas is by listing. You make a grocery list or a to do list. One of the things about a list is that it is not in alphabetical order, chronological order, or any other order usually. It is in the order that things pop into your mind, and for most of us, that means they come very randomly. So the first thing on your list might not have anything to do with the next thing.

For example, imagine a shopping list. The first thing you put on there might be coffee because you ran out this morning. But you have creamer and sugar, so those don't go on there, but you might remember right then that you put the last toilet paper roll in the toilet paper holder this morning. So, coffee is right next to toilet paper on the list. They don't have anything to do with each other except for the fact that you need to buy them.

That's okay. Just list as many things as you can. At this point, you're coming up with ideas. Remember what we said about freewriting—don't worry about spelling, punctuation, anything. You're just getting ideas down on paper.

So, if we were trying to come up with a list of animals that make good pets, it might look something like this:

Dogs
Cats
Parakeets
Rottweiler
Collie
Siamese
Parrot
Bird

Persian
Tabby
Cockatiel
Chihuahua

IV. Clustering

Also called MAPPING, this method is often used by writers who do not like to be restricted to the linear listing or outlining methods. It often works better for creative, artistic, or technical writers. You start with one idea in the middle of a blank page and circle it. When your brain comes up with a related word, simply write it near the first one, circle it, and connect the two with a line. Then you can either connect more related words to the original word or connect related words to the words branching off the original.

V. Questioning

Asking yourself questions about what you know in regard to a topic is a long-held tradition in journalism. In fact, the main questions asked by most people to generate ideas are referred to as the "Reporters' Questions" or "The Five W's" (plus one H). They are:

- Who?
- What?
- When?
- Where?
- Why?
- How?

In addition to these questions, come up with your own:

- What do I know about _____?
- What would I like to know?
- Where can I get more information?
- What would I like to focus on?

By thinking about the answers to these questions, you can begin to get an idea of what you know about the topic and what you don't. For a research paper, you could then look up information about the topic; for placement tests, you may want to focus on the areas you DO know something about.

VI. Keeping a Journal

Keeping a journal is another way of generating ideas for when your instructor wants you to come up with your own topic. The journal entries for most people are merely regular freewriting sessions. Don't worry about your punctuation, grammar, or spelling in the journal. This is a place to let your mind roam in search of topics it wants to think about. Of course, you can use the journal to focus on topics you have been given in order to come up with information and details about those topics.

Learning Activity

Try different ways of generating ideas for your three points. If one doesn't work, try another. The two I've found to work most often for students and for me are clustering (or mapping) and freewriting. Freewriting has been the most beneficial of all these in my career as a professional writer. It keeps you from getting writer's block.

First, fill in the next three boxes in each template with ideas that help support the topic sentence in the top box of each template. The following is an outline that shows what that should look like.

Example

by major   by time   by instructor

_____   _____   _____

_____   _____   _____

Second, they are free from parental involvement:

when to come in   where you can go   friends

_____   _____   _____

_____   _____   _____

Third, they are responsible for their own actions:

getting up on time   attendance   studying

_____   _____   _____

_____   _____   _____

NOTES:

Unit One: Prewriting
Part 2 - Organizing Ideas

Organizing Ideas

Once you've come up with a bunch of ideas about a topic, you need a way to organize those ideas. We will use this later in the unit on Using the Thesis Statement to Organize Your Paragraph.

There are three very common ways to organize ideas:

1. Outline
2. Mapping
3. Template

Outline

An outline is nothing more than an organized list. Say we had a list of animals that make good pets:

Dogs
Cats
Birds
Siamese
Rottweiler
Collie
Parrot
Persian
Chihuahua
Parakeet
Cockatiel
Tabby

If we take that list and try to find all the major groups of animals within that list, we can come up with several:

Dogs
Cats
Birds

Then, if we look at the list and try to find each animal that fits under that group, we get an outline:

Dogs
Siamese
Collie
Chihuahua

Cats
Siamese
Persian
Tabby

Birds
Parrot
Parakeet
Cockatiel

A lot of people are turned off to outlining because of the rigid rules you had in high school like when to use I., II., III.; when to use 1., 2., 3.; or that you couldn't have a 1. without a 2. or an A. without a B.

For our purposes here, that is not an issue. An outline is a tool, and sometimes teachers forget that. They become a test or an assessment, and their entire value is based on whether you get the outline correct according a big set of rules.

All I want you to worry about when using an outline for a tool is that you can tell exactly what items go under what categories. As long as you can tell that Rottweiler, Collie, and Chihuahua are all dogs, I'm happy. What you're doing is just figuring out what goes with what. You're grouping your ideas into categories that go together. You won't put Parakeet under dogs because it doesn't go there. Parakeets go under birds, so put them there.

Cluster

Clustering is also called mapping or spiderwebbing. We talked about it in Generating Ideas. Where that one was branching out all over the place, the one we'd like to use for organizing ideas is a little simpler. If we had a cluster of the same animals as we did above in outline, we could make a cluster something like this:

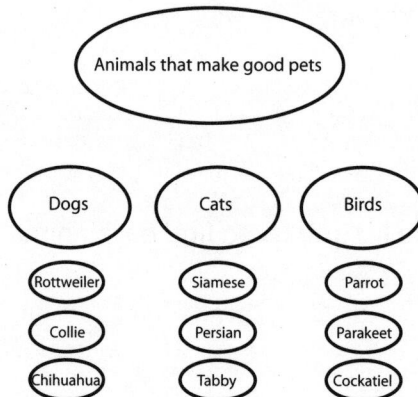

Again, this gives us some idea of how we're going to group the ideas together to make sense to the reader.

Template

A slightly different version of the cluster is the template in the appendices and again in the unit *Using the Thesis Statement to Organize Your Essay*. It looks something like this:

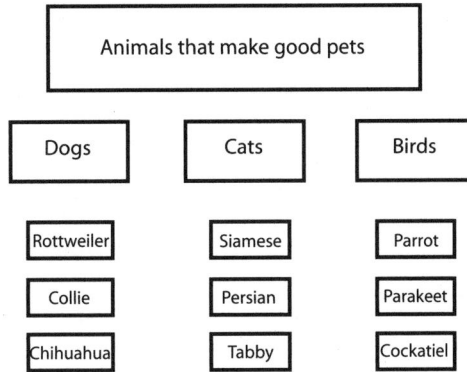

```
            ┌─────────────────────────────────┐
            │   Animals that make good pets    │
            └─────────────────────────────────┘

     ┌──────────┐      ┌──────────┐      ┌──────────┐
     │   Dogs   │      │   Cats   │      │  Birds   │
     └──────────┘      └──────────┘      └──────────┘

     ┌──────────┐      ┌──────────┐      ┌──────────┐
     │ Rottweiler│     │ Siamese  │      │  Parrot  │
     └──────────┘      └──────────┘      └──────────┘
     ┌──────────┐      ┌──────────┐      ┌──────────┐
     │  Collie  │      │ Persian  │      │ Parakeet │
     └──────────┘      └──────────┘      └──────────┘
     ┌──────────┐      ┌──────────┐      ┌──────────┐
     │ Chihuahua│      │  Tabby   │      │ Cockatiel│
     └──────────┘      └──────────┘      └──────────┘
```

For some reason, the template seems to work for a lot of writers who aren't comfortable with the outline or cluster. Later we'll see how we use these "organizational plans" to write a paragraph or an essay.

NOTES:

Unit Two:
Organization of an Essay

This unit will help you to understand how an effective essay should be organized. It will provide examples and activities to help you understand this organization.

Learning Objectives

At the end of this unit, you will:

1. understand the organization of an effective essay;

2. be able to produce an informal, but effective outline of an essay; and

3. understand that this organization is the same for paragraphs, essays, term papers, and longer reports.

Organization of an Essay

An essay is organized into three separate sections: the introduction, body (made up of the major points), and conclusion:

1. Introduction
2. Body
    a. Point one
    b. Point two
    c. Point three
3. Conclusion

This organization will work for all levels of writing, whether an eight-sentence paragraph, a five-paragraph essay, a ten-page paper, a fifty-page thesis, or a 200,000-page report on O-ring failure in a space shuttle. Only the amount of information will change for each of these.

Wilhite's Writing Wisdom:

The introduction of a paragraph will be only one sentence: a topic sentence. The topic sentence is the key to the organization of the remainder of the paragraph. The thesis statement is the most important part of an essay.

For the essay, the introduction consists of an introductory paragraph, which includes a thesis statement (the essay equivalent of a topic sentence). Persuasive writing means that you are trying to get your audience to understand (not necessarily buy into) your opinion by presenting them with several points that support your opinion. Those points are then supported by proofs that show why that point is valid.

People throughout history have used a similar method to persuade other people to buy things. Salesmen in all their forms have used the technique of **"Tell 'em** what you're going to tell 'em, **tell 'em**, then **tell 'em** what you told 'em." Politicians and sportscasters, as well as everyone in between, still use this method to get their points across.

Take, for example, a State of the Union address by the President. Although the address starts at seven p.m., political analysts take over the television screen at about six or six-thirty p.m. Why? To tell us what they expect the President to discuss in his address:

> *"Well, Bill, the President will almost surely talk about national budget. After all, that more than anything else affects the State of the Union, unless we are at war."*

> *"Right, Dan. And speaking of war, defense will be one of the top priorities of this address in an effort to keep us out of the Middle East fracas."*

> *"Absolutely. And the President said just yesterday that the ability of the United States to stay ahead of other countries in defense is tied to increased education for the American people."*

> *"Yes. And that brings us right back to the budget."*

Then the President comes on. He tells us that the national budget has some severe problems and talks about those problems and how he plans to introduce legislation that will alleviate them. He talks about defense and how the military must increase the number of tanks and airplanes it has and how much each one costs. He talks about needing more educated people in America to make more money, pay more taxes, and increase the amount of money the government has to buy things as well as be educated enough to use the more advanced weapons and technologies that will be involved.

Then the analysts come back on to tell us what the President said because, of course, we are not bright enough to figure out what he just told us, right? No. Because they want to make sure that the message sticks. In effect, the President has just used the "Tell 'em, tell 'em, tell 'em" technique to sell us on his proposed legislation for the next year. Or at least to make us understand why he is doing it.

An even more common example of this technique is an NFL football game. If the game is scheduled to start at noon, what happens at eleven a.m.? The pre-game show.

Howard Cosell and Dandy Don Meredith (yes, I'm showing my age, but they were the most fun to listen to of all sports commentators) came on an hour before the game to tell us what? Who is going to play, what strengths and weaknesses each team has, how those will affect today's game, and how they expect to see it go:

> *"Howard, Dallas is really going to miss Michael Runaway today."*

> *"That's right, Don. We'll see John Wilson filling in for him, and Wilson is an unknown who is supposed to have excellent hands but who will be appearing in his first pro game today."*

> *"Well, we'll be watching to see what happens there. Of course, Dallas has signed a new placekicker, Yon Bigleg, who is supposed to have a cannon for a right leg. We've heard unsubstantiated reports that he can split the uprights from close to 100 yards away. On the other side, the Redskins' quarterback is having a tremendous season, having completed ninety percent of his passes to their new wide receiver, Jerry Catchalot. And running back Mike Ballhandler beat the season rushing record this year in the first game of the season and has now tallied more than 5,000 yards with half a season to go still. It will be an interesting game to say the least."*

Then the game comes on.

Sure enough, John Wilson makes some amazing leaps and dives to get his hands on the ball, catching twenty-eight passes during the first quarter. But, just as amazing, he fumbles twenty-seven of them. The Redskins take each of those fumbles in for a touchdown (TD) and point-after-touchdown (PAT) to score 189 points. To add to that, Catchalot pulls in thirty passes for six TDs and PATs to up the Washington score to 231. And Ballhandler runs for five more TDs, but the kicker is so tired that he misses all the PATs, bringing Washington's total to 261.

Dallas's only highlights are provided by field goal kicker Yon Bigleg, who begins the second quarter, after the coach pulls Catchalot at the end of the first quarter, by kicking a field goal on the first play from scrimmage each time Dallas gets the ball. Bigleg kicks for a total of eleven field goals, the shortest one being eighty-five yards and the longest one from his own goal line, for a total of thirty-three points.

The game ends: Dallas 33, Washington 261.

Now that the game has ended, the channel will return to cartoons or something, right? I don't think so. What comes after the game?

The post-game show, of course!

The post-game show recaps the action from the game, providing us with the highlights to remember.

If we just wanted to know who would be playing, we could watch the pre-game show (introduction). If we just wanted to know who won and the highlights, we could watch the post-game show or the sports highlights on the news later (conclusion). But even with both of those available to us, we watch the game.

Why?

For the details. That is what the body gives us. We already know what the main points are going to be, but we watch the game to see the details of how those points are accomplished. Later when someone talks about Dallas's loss, we know all the details:

> *"Sure, Catchalot fumbled twenty-seven times, but did you see those twenty-eight catches? If we can just get him to hang on to the ball … wow! And what about that Bigleg? He could launch a rocket to the moon."*

So, we see the value of this structure. The introduction tells us what to expect and what to watch out for in the main event. The body gives us those signposts and then tells us additional details that we need to know to be knowledgeable about the subject. The conclusion reminds us of the key points or highlights right before we leave.

How effective is this technique? Ask any football fan and listen to him quote the highlights of the game he watched Sunday afternoon or Monday night. And watch to see how those highlights are expanded upon as he recalls the details of the actual game as he saw them. Knowing what to watch for allows us to pick up other information during the game, the details we need to make intelligent comments about the game.

Just as the pre-game show tells us the key elements to watch for in the upcoming game, the thesis statement tells us what to expect from the coming essay. Then, when those points are made again, the reader begins to believe in the writer (the reliable narrator). By knowing the "highlights" that should be coming, the reader is able to concentrate more on the details when they appear and able to recall more of the information when finished.

Therefore, the introduction (thesis statement at the essay level) is the key to writing effective paragraphs, speeches, sales pitches, or instructions on how to call wild geese or fix a bicycle tire.

Learning Activity

During the next week, watch for a sporting event, political event, or other event on TV that fits the above organization. Take note of how it breaks down into an introduction, the main event, and a conclusion. Write a couple of sentences telling what the event you watched was and how these three main parts were evident.

Example #1

I watched a campaign speech by Joe Smith for Congress. For the intro, he talked about the three areas that he is good at—finance, politics, and honesty. For the body, he gave a lot of information and details about each of those areas. He told how he had been a banker for twenty years, how he had been a state representative for ten years, and how he had returned a million dollars when he found it in the street. For the conclusion, he reminded everyone that he was good at finance, good at politics, and honest.

Example #2

I watched the news. For the intro, they talked about the three top stories—one from local news, one from the weather, and one from sports. For the body, they gave the details about each story. They told how a local man is raising asparagus in just a tub of water with no dirt, how the excessive flooding in south Texas has hurt peanut production and stalled trucks delivering food, and how the rumored baseball strike has really ticked off baseball fans. For the conclusion, they reminded us that a Waco man is raising crops with twenty-first century technology, how we won't have any peanuts for a few months because of the weather, and how baseball fans are turning to high school and college sports rather than pro baseball.

NOTES:

Unit Three:
Thesis Statements

This unit will help you to understand how an effective thesis statement provides the basis for the organization of an essay or paragraph.

Learning Objectives

At the end of this unit, you will:

1. be able to identify the elements of an effective thesis statement;

2. understand where the elements of an effective thesis statement can be found in a writing prompt; and

3. be able to produce an effective thesis statement.

Thesis Statements

As stated at the end of the second unit (Organization Of An Essay), the thesis statement is the key to an organized, well-written essay, especially with placement tests such as the Texas Higher Education Assessment (THEA) test or the Accuplacer. In the THEA, you will be writing an essay from a prompt you have never seen. By following the instructions ahead, you will be shown an easy way to find most, if not all, of the information you need for the thesis statement of your essay. Done correctly, this sentence will practically write much of the essay for you.

The thesis statement is made up of three parts:

THE TOPIC + YOUR OPINION + POINTS ONE, TWO, AND THREE

The topic is the main idea of what you are writing about. You usually get the topic from a prompt or a test question.

Example prompt:

As a college freshman, you have just finished four years of high school. You are now embarking on your college studies. Many freshmen say that college is just a continuation of high school for them, with the same kinds of topics, same kinds of classrooms, and same kinds of teachers. Others say that college is a completely new experience in education for them, saying they are free to pick classes, free from parental involvement, and responsible for their own actions. Is attending college different from going to high school?

To find the topic, read the ENTIRE prompt. Then, look for the question and turn it into a statement.

Is attending college different from going to high school?

The question is asking you to make a decision: attending college IS/IS NOT different from going to high school. YOU have to decide if college is different or not.

For purposes of this lesson, let's say that YOU think college is different. Now you can make a definite statement:

Attending college IS different from going to high school.

You have made the first step in coming up with a thesis statement. You've made the decision of which way your essay is headed. You need to do a couple of things to make it a complete thesis statement.

First, add "because" to your statement. That should give you the following statement:

Attending college is different from going to high school because

Next, give three good points (reasons) that show college is different from high school. (This will really help you when you begin writing your essay.) These are the one, two, and three in the formula above.

You are not entirely alone in this quest for points, however. Use the prompt or test question for any help it can give you. For example, this prompt tells you that many students think college "is a completely new experience in education" and then lists three points that support that decision. Take those three points (free to pick classes, free from parental involvement, and responsible for their own actions) and add them to the statement you made, placing them after the word "because."

You may have to change the points a little to make them make sense. Read the statement you formed from the question (with "because" at the end of it) and attach each of the points to it. For example, "Attending college is different from going to high school because free to pick classes." That doesn't sound quite right because the point you added doesn't say who has this freedom. Sometimes, you have to change the point slightly to make it fit on the end of the statement. You could have solved this by picking up the "they are" along with the first point.

However, because your thesis statement is the opening for YOUR essay, the reader doesn't know who "they" are. Remember that you can't count on a reader having read the prompt. The prompt is just the reason you are writing the essay. Fortunately, just a slight change makes the sentence fit perfectly— "Attending college is different from going to high school because college students are free to pick classes."

Do this for the second and third points and you have your thesis statement in finished form:

> *Attending college is different from going to high school because college students are free to pick classes, free from parental involvement, and responsible for their own actions.*

Wilhite's Writing Wisdom:

Make sure that the three points are separated by commas, especially with a comma before the "and" between the second and third points.

Now that you have a thesis statement, you'll need to come up with details to support the points you have chosen as proof of your opinion. You may want to freewrite, map (cluster), list, or outline your thoughts on each of the points to help you generate ideas for such support. We'll talk about those things in a later lesson.

But first, let's recap the five-step process for coming up with a thesis statement. You will:

1. find the question;

2. make a decision;

3. turn the question into a statement;

4. add "because"; and

5. pull your three points from the prompt.

(You may encounter prompts that do not have your three points in them. The idea-generating techniques we'll discuss in a later lesson will help with that. But for right now, we're working with prompts that DO have the three points in them.)

You will also note that we are copying as much information from the prompt as possible. Use your prompt in this way to make sure you do not get off topic. There is no problem at this point in copying the exact phrases from the prompt, as long as they fit together to make a sentence. In fact, using the same words ensures you are not using an incorrect word. There will be plenty of other places within your essay to use different words for the same things. Also, the prompt is a good place to check your spelling, since you won't have a spell check when you are taking standardized tests (like the THEA or Accuplacer), in-class exams, or finals.

Learning Activity

If you followed along with the above process, you should now have a thesis statement for an essay describing how college is different from high school.

(Be sure that you understand where each part of the thesis statement came from. IF YOU DO NOT UNDERSTAND WHERE EACH PART CAME FROM AND HOW THEY ALL GO TOGETHER, GO BACK THROUGH THE PROCESS UNTIL YOU DO. If you have gone back through the process a couple of times and still don't understand, ask for help from an instructor or tutor, or post a message to a discussion board.)

Unit Four:
Using the Thesis Statement to Organize Your Essay

This unit will help you to understand how the essay can be organized from a well-written thesis statement.

Learning Objective

At the end of this unit, you will:

1. be able to produce sentences that clearly state the points to be made in support of the thesis statement.

Using the Thesis Statement to Organize Your Essay

Now, we'll pull the organization part section and the thesis statement section together.

Your thesis statement now has all the information you need to produce three clear sentences that provide the "points" you will support in your essay.

When you are handwriting the thesis statement in the pre-writing stage, you can put numbers in parentheses at the beginning of each of your points. Handwritten, you can do this by writing the number above the sentence and circling it. This will not appear in your final copy, but is to help you make sure you do, in fact, have three points and allow you to keep them straight in this next phase.

Now, take the first number—(1)—and "bring it down" to start a new paragraph immediately after the thesis statement. However, instead of writing "(1)" you will write "First," to start this new paragraph. This is a transition and lets the reader know that you are now going to talk about the first point you mentioned in the thesis statement.

The next thing you will do is copy the phrase from the first point down immediately after "First," making this the topic sentence for your second paragraph. This will become the "point one" back in your organizational chart.

A big danger here, and with each of the following points, is that the phrase from the thesis statement may not be a complete sentence. "First, you pick your own classes" is indeed a complete sentence. However, "First, are free to pick the classes you need or want" would not be a complete sentence.

> ***Wilhite's Writing Wisdom:***
>
> Make sure that each of these "point" sentences is, in fact, a complete sentence. This is one of the most common places for sentence fragments to occur. Always double check your "First," "Second," and "Third" sentences to be sure they are not fragments.

You will later do the same for the second and third points, but right now, your essay should look like this:

Attending college is different from going to high school because college students are free to pick classes, free from parental involvement, and responsible for their own actions.

First, college students are free to pick classes.

Right now, you are probably saying to yourself, "But that's exactly what I said in the sentence right before this. My teachers always said not to repeat myself like that."

In this case, don't worry about it. This is just one step in the process. The repetitive sentences will eventually be far enough away from each other that each will serve as a reminder for the reader. Right now, it does look awkward, but don't let it worry you here.

Now that you have these two sentences written down, let's move on to how you come up with details to support this point and the other two to follow.

Learning Activity

Add the sentence you've written in this unit to your thesis statement.

Unit Five:
Planning the Rough Draft

This unit will show you how to use a template to plan your essay and produce the rough draft.

Learning Objective

At the end of this unit, you will:

1. be able to produce a template for each body paragraph.

Planning The Rough Draft

Now, you are going to learn to make and use a Paragraph Organization Template where you will simply transfer your three points from the thesis statement onto blank Paragraph Organization Templates.

Take out three blank sheets of paper and turn them sideways. Draw a long horizontal box at the top of each page. Under that box, draw three columns of three boxes each. Stack the three sheets of paper on top of one another.

On the first page, write "First" in the top box. Then, on the second page, write "Second" in the top box, and on the third page, write "Third" in the top box.

Now, write your three points from the thesis statement in each of the three top boxes. You should have something that looks the diagram on the following page.

Point #1

First, students are free to pick their own classes.

SPECIFIC: How? Why?

DETAILS & EXAMPLES

Point #2

Second, students are free from parental involvement.

SPECIFIC: How? Why?

DETAILS & EXAMPLES

Point #3

Third, students are responsible for their own actions.

SPECIFIC: How? Why?

DETAILS & EXAMPLES

> ***Wilhite's Writing Wisdom:***
>
> It may seem counterintuitive to do so much prep work before you write the essay itself. But, just think to how a house is built: carpenters don't start with a pile of boards and figure out how the house will look as they go. Instead, they follow thoughtfully conceived plans to make sure the finished product is as polished and good looking as possible.

Right now, we need to discuss some ways to help you come up with ideas for the body as well as the kinds of ideas to come up with and how to put them in order and tie the whole paper together.

Learning Activity

From Unit Four, you should be able to make three sentences from your thesis. Write these three in the Paragraph Organization Template. Using the template, make a sentence for each box (three main point sentences you should already have and then two sentences of detail about each of those points). We'll fill in the conclusion box later. Then copy these sentences out in paragraph form for your rough draft.

<u>Example</u>

Sorry folks. I'm not going to give you an example here. You're now on your own.

NOTES:

Unit Six:
Achieving Coherence & Unity

This unit will present several ways of organizing your ideas in your essay as well as within the paragraphs making up your essay.

Learning Objectives

At the end of this unit, you will:

1. understand how to produce a unified essay;

2. understand the difference between time order, space order, and order of importance; and

3. understand how related sentences help keep an essay unified.

Achieving Coherence & Unity

You've probably heard the root word of coherence in such phrases as "a coherent whole" or "a cohesive unit." This should give you some idea of its meaning. Coherence simply means that an essay should work as one whole unit.

Wilhite's Writing Wisdom:

Everything in the essay MUST WORK TOGETHER to get across the main idea (or thesis) of the essay.

There are a couple of ways of "tying the essay together." First, you can place the main points in some sort of order that makes sense to the reader and lets him know that all the elements in the essay belong together by how they fit in the essay. Second, you can use repetition of key points, ideas, phrases, and words so that the reader sees how these repeated elements tie all of the sentences to the thesis or main idea.

Coherence & Unity Through Order

There are three ways of placing your ideas in order in your paper. Order merely means which ideas will come first, which second, and which third.

I. Time Order

A common method of ordering ideas in a paper is to put them in time (chronological) order. This means moving from the past to the present or from present to past. You just put ideas down on paper in the order that they naturally occur. Words that help create this order are first, second, then, next, before, during, after, soon, while, when, suddenly, later, and finally.

II. Space Order

Another way to arrange ideas is space order. Space order is used to move the reader's imaginary eye from detail to detail, like in a movie. The imaginary eye travels left to right, top to bottom, or from foreground to background. Words that convey this idea of movement in space include *left, right, top, bottom, up, down, over, under, on top of, below, beside, next to, behind,* and *alongside.*

III. Order Of Importance

In many cases, such as answers to essay questions, you will probably want to arrange ideas in their order of importance. This can be from most important to least important, or it can be from least important to most important. Putting the most important idea first makes sure that the reader is aware of it very early in the paper. This can be very important if your audience needs to have the important idea quickly. On the other hand, some audiences respond best when the least important ideas come first, leading up to the most important point. Words that are used to express the importance of one idea over another include *first, next, above all, even more, especially, most important, least of all, most of all,* and *last.*

Moving from the most important to least important point also helps us understand the idea of going from general to specific.

If you ever read a newspaper article about a wreck, the order goes something like this:

> *One dies in I-35 wreck.*

That headline tells you what happened, so you've got the most important point: someone was killed in a wreck on I-35. But you can go into more detail about EACH element in this headline. Let's start with the "One" of the headline:

_____*One*_____

_____*a man* _____

_____*from Waco* _____

_____*a lawyer* _____

___*Joe Jones of 123 Main St.*___

If each sentence in the following story gives a little more information—a little more SPECIFIC information—about the person, you are starting with some anonymous person (*one*) who could be ANYONE in the whole world. Then you go to a man (more specific—HALF of the people in the whole world.) Then to *from Waco* (more specific—maybe only 50,000 male citizens of Waco). Then you give his occupation of *lawyer* (more specific—maybe only 100 male lawyers in Waco). And finally you come to *Joe Jones* and 123 Main St. (very specific—only one person by that name at that address).

Okay, maybe there's a Joe Jones, Joe Jones Jr., and a Joe Jones III living at that address, but that's when you'd need to get even MORE specific and give the "Jr." or "III" or maybe an age. That's why you always see newspapers with sentences like:

> *Joe Jones Jr., 48, of 123 Main St., son of billionaire Joe Jones and father of Dallas Cowboys star running back Joe Jones III, died in a wreck on I-35 yesterday.*

Now there is absolutely no question about WHO died or about which of the Jones men it was. This is called the inverted pyramid and is taught to journalists in their very first class.

I really like this order of most important to least important or general to specific because it helps the reader immensely as he tries to follow the story. Let's look at another example that shows WHY this is important.

Let's say that I came into class and walked up to one of my students, Steve. I'm really excited about something that happened on the way to school. I might say something like this:

"Steve, man, you should have seen the wreck I saw coming into school. I was headed down the freeway and as I got to that big overpass just before the exit for school, this little old lady in a Yugo was in the right lane as a semi-truck in the left lane moved over. Pushed her little car right through the guardrail and she flew off the freeway and landed in that Beer N Gas store there on the service road. Her car went through the gas pumps, shattered the front glass doors, scattered the potato chip rack, and ran right through the beer cooler doors.

"Dude, there was gas spewing all over the place, beer spraying on everything, and potato chips falling like snow. It was absolutely amazing!

"Oh, yeah, and by the way, it was your mother."

Now, I don't think Steve would be real happy with me right then. Why? Because I gave him all the details in a long story before I got to the most important part. He would much rather I walked straight up to him and said, "Steve, your mom's been in a wreck, but she's okay." This way, he has the most important information up front. As soon as that important information is out of the way, he will probably THEN ask, "What in the world happened?" Now he's ready for the details, so I'd say, "Dude, it was absolutely amazing, this semi …"

By and large, most people in the world want the most important information up front and the details later. Think of how many times you have heard someone say "Get to the point" when someone else is droning on and on about something, but the listener can't figure out what the point of the conversation is. So, we're going to work on giving readers the general information first and then filling in the specific details later.

Coherency Through Related Sentences

Order is not the only way to tie an essay together, but it does give the reader some idea of how the essay might be organized. Once the reader has that information, then the writer can help the reader again by using words that keep his sentences related. This means that there's something in one sentence that allows the reader to see how that sentence leads to—or connects to—the next one. We'll use paragraphs to show this because they're smaller, but the same concept applies to essays as well.

I. Repetition

Repeating important words, phrases, and ideas help to link the sentences together. For example, a paragraph on a *grand jury indictment* might include the words grand jury, jury, and indictment several times to keep the reader focused on the topic of the paragraph:

> *Yesterday the grand jury issued an indictment against Joe Thomas*
> *for burglary of a residence. The grand jury heard statements from the*
> *defense attorney and the prosecution. The jury decided there was enough*
> *information to indict Thomas on the charges. The indictment was issued at*
> *2:45 p.m.*

II. Synonyms & Substitutions

To avoid overuse of a particular word, a writer can use synonyms (words that mean nearly the same thing) and substitutions (other words that describe the subject). An essay could use *building* in the first sentence, *bank* in the second, and *edifice* in the third sentence. These are all synonyms that mean the same thing. The pronoun *it* could also substituted for the word *building.*

III. Transitional Expressions

Transitions also help hold an essay together. They can point out the exact relation between one idea and another or one sentence and another. They help to keep the reader going in the right direction. Here's an example:

> *Cars used to be gas-guzzling monsters. However, recent advances in motor*
> *design, aerodynamics, and transmissions have created smaller cars, which*
> *get gas mileage nearly double that of cars ten years ago. As a result, a new*
> *car buyer can now expect gas mileage of thirty mpg from many mid-size*
> *vehicles. For example, the new Hyundai Sonata gets thirty-two mpg and*
> *provides room for five adults.*

In the above, the first sentence that says *Cars used to be gas-guzzling monsters.* If the next sentence starts with the transition words *However,* then the transition word introduces the idea that this is changing. *As a result,* which introduces the following sentence, makes it clear that the sentence coming is based on the previous sentence: *recent advances have resulted in thirty mpg cars.* In the next sentence, *for example* shows one specific illustration of a one particular car that is an example of thirty mpg cars.

Learning Activity

Look at the transitions we have used to move from one point to the next ("First,""Second,""Third," or "Last,") in your essay. These often indicate time order. But note that YOU are the one that chooses which one the reader is asked to consider first, second, and third. So, YOU determine the order of importance. You may want them in order from least important to most important, or you may want them in order from most important to least important. YOU make that decision. YOU are the writer. YOU decide the best order for your information.

Also, notice how repetition is used by repeating the key phrases from the thesis statement again in the topic sentence. You will probably use synonyms and substitution when presenting the details to your three main points. For example, when talking about classes you want, you won't want to continue to say "classes" by itself in the next few sentences. You might use synonyms like courses or subjects in the next sentences. Or you might use substitutions like algebra or English.

Use transitions ("First, …", "Second, …", and "Third, …" for the major point, or topic sentence, of each paragraph; "One …", "Another …", and "One more …" for the sub-points in each paragraph; and "For example, …" for each example) to indicate to your reader that you are moving from one point and/or example to another.

Unit Seven: Persuasion

This unit will discuss methods of persuasive writing.

Learning Objective

At the end of this unit, you will:

1. understand the various methods used in persuasive writing.

Persuasive Writing

Any time you try to persuade someone, you are trying to convince him that your opinion, your point of view, or your assessment is correct or that it is, at least, valid.

Arguments with your friends and family, television commercials, and advertisements are all forms of persuasive argument. Each is trying to get its message across to its audience (your friends, your family, TV viewers, magazine readers) in order to convince that audience to either change its opinion or at least accept the other opinion as having some value.

Much of writing in college is persuasive writing. You may try to convince your history instructor that these ARE the main causes of the Civil War or your auto mechanics instructor that these ARE the basic steps in rebuilding the transmission in a Chevy truck. In your career, if you write a memo to your boss asking for a raise, you will be trying to persuade him that you deserve one.

In all of these, you will have to prove, back up, or *support* your arguments. That support will come from citing specific details about the causes of the Civil War, rebuilding a transmission, or your job performance.

In a persuasive argument, you are expected to provide points that support your argument. And, typically, your reader usually expects three such points to be convinced. If you were writing a paper to convince me that you did, indeed, deserve a raise at work, I would want to see at least three points that prove you DO deserve it. For example, you might cite:

1. an important project that you have completed recently;

2. new responsibilities you have taken upon yourself; and

3. an increase in sales over the last few months.

You would then provide detailed information about each of these points to convince me that you deserve the raise. In the above example, you could discuss the important project you completed:

> *The recent poster translation project I was in charge of was completed sixty days ahead of schedule. This speedy completion saved the company $12,000 by allowing staff to proceed to a second project that we would have turned down if we hadn't completed the poster job early.*

You would then do the same for the remaining two points that support your request for a raise.

Methods of Persuasion

There are many different methods of persuasion. Now we'll look at six of them: *facts, referring to an authority, examples, predicting the consequences, answering the opposition, and considering the audience.*

I. Facts

Facts are merely statements of what is, not opinion, and should include a source. For example, you might want to prove that children's eyesight should be checked annually by an eye doctor. Facts about this could come from an eye industry magazine:

> *Many people suffer serious visual impairment later in life because they received insufficient or inadequate eye care when they were children, according to an article in* Better Vision.

You want to avoid vague sources, such as "people say" or "everyone knows." These make your reader doubt your sources.

II. Referring to an Authority

An authority is someone who is considered to be an expert. Experts are people who provide unbiased facts and information upon a subject. For instance, a doctor is a person most people expect to provide them with all the information—good and bad—about a medical condition, treatment, or cure. You could use a quote from a doctor to support your point that "smoking is dangerous." You could also use materials from the American Medical Association or the American Lung Association to support that same point.

One of the problems with modern advertising is its use of celebrities to endorse products. While Michael Jordan is, indeed, an expert on basketball, he may not be a good expert to quote in support of buying auto insurance.

III. Examples

An example is a specific event that demonstrates your point is true. It supports your argument by showing how a specific incident proves your point. For example, to support the point that high schools should provide more funds for women's sports, you could use an example:

> *Jefferson High School, for instance, has received inquiries from sixty female students who would be willing to join a women's basketball or baseball team if the school could provide the uniforms, the space, and a coach.*

IV. Predicting the Consequences

When you predict the consequences, you help the reader visualize what will occur if something does or does not happen. If you want to convince your reader that all qualified students deserve a free education, you could make a prediction:

> *If bright but economically deprived students cannot attend college because they cannot afford it, our society will be robbed of their talents.*

Be sure, however, that you do not exaggerate the consequences:

> *If you don't eat fresh fruit every day, you will never be healthy.*

V. Answering the Opposition

When the opposition has a particularly well-known argument, an exceptionally effective strategy is to state that argument and then give your answer to it. This assures the reader that you are aware of the opposition and its argument and that you have an answer for the argument:

> *Some have criticized him for running a low-key campaign, but he feels that the issues and his stand on them speak for themselves.*

VI. Considering the Audience

Another thing to consider when writing a persuasive argument is the audience. Obviously, you would not write the same letter to the president of your college requesting a longer spring break that you would write to your best friend discussing why you would like a longer spring break. Not only would your style of writing be more formal in the letter to the president, your arguments would also be different:

Dear President Stuckly:

The students at Texas State Technical College feel that a longer spring break would allow them additional time to complete spring term papers, to prepare for the rigors of studying for finals, and to hold study groups to better internalize the extensive technical data they are exposed to daily.

Dear Joe:

I think we need a longer spring break so that we can catch a whole lot more really good waves, work on our tans, and find those girls we met last year in Miami Beach.

Wilhite's Writing Wisdom:

In general, you may want to avoid using the "Predicting the Consequences" or the "Answering the Opposition" methods of persuasion for THEA or other writing placement tests. Too often, students using these two methods get confused halfway (or earlier) through their essay and end up actually arguing against themselves. It is just too easy to do with these particular methods.

Learning Activity

Fill in the boxes in your template, using the above kinds of information. For the purpose of in-class, off-the-top-of-your-head essays, your best bets are probably facts and examples. The facts and examples you use in class do not have to be absolutely accurate like they would in a research paper. You're coming up with them off the top of your head, so they may not be correct.

For example, you might write:

A study by the American Association of Freshman Students shows that seventy percent of all incoming freshman in college fail at least one class.

No one is going to track down whether such an organization exists or whether the seventy-percent figure is correct. But you are showing the instructor that you know the KIND of information you should put in that spot. For a research paper or freshman composition paper, you would be looking that information up to make sure it was correct. For a test essay, that information would be the stuff that you had been studying in the chapters of the textbook before the test.

Unit Eight:
The Conclusion

This unit will help you to understand how the conclusion can be formed from a well-written thesis statement.

Learning Objective

At the end of this unit, you will:

1. be able to produce a clear conclusion.

The Conclusion

This can (and should be) the simplest part of the entire process. After all, everything you need for your conclusion has already been done for you, right? All you have to do is copy the information again and change the order of it.

So where is all this information?

Right back in that all-important thesis statement:

> *Attending college is different from going to high school because college students are free to pick classes they need or want, free from parental involvement, and responsible for their own actions.*

First, I want you to break the thesis statement into two parts, cutting it in front of the word "because":

1. *Attending college is different from going to high school*

2. *because college students are free to pick classes they need or want, free from parental involvement, and responsible for their own actions.*

Now, all you do is switch the two parts:

1. *because college students are free to pick classes they need or want, free from parental involvement, and responsible for their own actions.*

2. *Attending college is different from going to high school*

Now, you have to make a couple of changes to make it a real sentence. Since all sentences begin with a capital letter, you need to capitalize "because":

Because college students are free to pick classes they need or want, free from parental involvement, and responsible for their own actions.

Next, you have to turn the period at the end into a comma because this is a dependent clause:

Because college students are free to pick classes they need or want, free from parental involvement, and responsible for their own actions,

Now, attach what was the beginning of the thesis statement to the end of this clause:

Because college students are free to pick classes they need or want, free from parental involvement, and responsible for their own actions, Attending college is different from going to high school

Of course, you don't have a capital letter in the middle of a sentence unless it is a proper name, so you need to make the "A" in "Attending" a lower-case letter. And, because all sentences have to end with a punctuation mark, you need to add a period at the end of the sentence:

Because college students are free to pick classes they need or want, free from parental involvement, and responsible for their own actions, attending college is different from going to high school.

As you can see, the actual process is simple, but leaving out any of the punctuation or capitalization would be a major problem. Simply put, here's all you do:

1. Break the topic sentence thesis statement into two parts right before the word "because."

2. Switch the two parts.

3. Make the necessary capitalization and punctuation changes. (Capitalize one lowercase, lowercase one capital, turn a period into a comma, and add a period at the end.)

That's it. You've made a perfectly acceptable conclusion. You've restated your main points and led straight from them into your main idea (your opinion on the topic) to effectively remind the reader that these reasons are why you think this particular way about the topic.

Wilhite's Writing Wisdom:

As a writing teacher it's easy to tell when a student has written a paper in one sitting with no pre-writing or revision because usually the conclusion makes a point unrelated to how the paper was set up in the introduction. Your introduction and conclusion MUST MATCH UP in terms of the overall point being made by the essay from beginning to end to achieve effective coherence and unity.

Learning Activity

Complete the conclusion paragraph for your essay.

NOTES:

Unit Nine: Writing the Final Draft

This unit will discuss revising the rough draft into a final draft.

Learning Objective

At the end of this unit, you will:

1. be able to revise a rough draft for unity and support.

Revising The Rough Draft

The next step in the writing process is revising your rough draft and turning it into a final draft. Revising merely means that you are going to rethink and rewrite your first draft, making whatever changes are needed to improve it.

> **Wilhite's Writing Wisdom:**
>
> THERE IS NOTHING SACRED ABOUT YOUR ROUGH DRAFT. You may change anything in it that needs to be changed. Add, drop, rearrange for clarification as necessary.

Ask yourself these questions, thinking about them from the reader's point of view:

- Is my thesis statement clear?

- Can the reader understand and follow my ideas easily?

- Does the essay follow a logical order and guide the reader from point to point?

Revising for Support

You will also check the essay's body paragraphs for adequate support—specific details, facts, and examples that help explain the topic sentences.

Revising for Unity

You must also check your essay for unity. You need to make sure that you do not drift away from the topic you are writing about. Sometimes, one of the supports gets so interesting or so involved that you may "take off on a tangent" on that support or some detail under it.

Say, for example, that you are doing an essay called "Dogs Make Wonderful Pets." Your supports are that "dogs give unconditional love, provide constant companionship, and are willing to put themselves in danger to save their masters."

When you get to the part about dogs saving their masters, you give an example of a collie that crawled through a fire to pull its master from the flames. So far, so good. But then you get sidetracked and start talking about a collie that you once had and how you had to put it to sleep when it got old and sick. You talk about how bad you felt when that happened.

At this point, you have gotten away from the point you were trying to make—how dogs will help save their owners—and onto another topic—how emotionally attached to their pets owners become. Had this been one of your points under the topic of dogs' making wonderful pets, fine. But it wasn't. So, you are off topic. This part of your paragraph is not "unified" or consistent with the rest of the paragraph. Your support does not prove your point.

Learning Activity

Look over your rough draft from the last lesson, reading it for unity and support. Again, if you have followed the process up to now, you won't find many errors in these areas. Make any changes necessary. Proofread and edit well (next unit). You need to compare your final draft with your rough draft to see what mistakes you found.

You will usually turn in your rough draft to your instructor at this stage— BEFORE proofreading and editing it. When you get the marked-up rough draft back, or if you put it on an overhead projector and go over it in class, OR if you sit down and go over it with the instructor, make sure you take note of what mistakes you made and how the instructor corrected them or suggested you correct them. Pull up your copy of the rough draft on your computer and MAKE the suggested corrections. This gets YOU in the habit of doing them and seeing them. In the next paper, maybe YOU will find those mistakes instead of your instructor.

This is to show you what kinds of mistakes YOU must look for in proofreading and editing your paper. The following unit will go over some of the most common mistakes that students make in grammar, punctuation, and spelling.

Unit Ten:
Proofreading & Editing

This unit will discuss the proofreading and editing process.

Learning Objective

At the end of this session, you will:

1. know which items to look for when proofreading an essay.

Proofreading & Editing

The final step in any writing—whether paragraph, essay, or term paper—is to proofread to find grammar, spelling, and punctuation errors and then correct them. This is the time to put your dictionary, thesaurus, and grammar book to use.

Unfortunately, many writers leave this step out. Often, students wait until the last minute, then try to write the paper the night before it is due. Even if they do the pre-writing (the other step usually skipped by many writers), they neglect the final proofreading to catch mistakes before turning the paper in.

Look up any words you even remotely think might be misspelled. Check for words you may have left out like *a, an, the, to, for,* or any helping verbs.

If you find any mistakes, correct them.

Top 10 Mistakes

1. fragments
2. run ons
3. comma splices
4. spelling
5. pronoun problems
6. point of view shifts
7. tense shifts
8. subject-verb agreement
9. introductory elements
10. commonly confused words

The Two Great Goofs (Most Common Essay Mistakes)

1. ORGANIZATION

Most beginning writers do not take time to organize their information or they organize it badly. Prewriting techniques like listing, questioning, mapping, freewriting, outlining, and using templates can help turn a writer's rambling mass of confusing information into a well-organized, easily understood essay. More information on this is in the Generating Ideas section.

2. PROOFREADING/EDITING

Another huge mistake beginning writers make is turning their essays in as soon as they put the last period in place. Writers need to take time to check their papers for mistakes in spelling, grammar, and punctuation.

Too often, they don't know what to look for. Information on what to look for is in the Top 10 Mistakes appendix and help on fixing those mistakes is in the appendices for each of the Top 10 Mistakes.

On a computer, run spell check and change the word to the correct spelling. (Hint: use your dictionary to look up the meaning of the words suggested as alternate spellings. This is not the time to guess. Make sure the spelling you think is correct means what you want the word to mean.) Once you have all the corrections made, print out a corrected copy of your paper.

If you have handwritten the paper, or if you are proofreading a typed paper in class before turning it in, make any corrections necessary as neatly as possible on the final draft.

Wilhite's Writing Wisdom:

There are many grammar, punctuation, and spelling books and Web sites out there. If you took a grammar class in the past and still have that grammar book, it might be easier to use it again since you know where things are in it.

Also, Strunk & White's *Elements of Style* is a handy little book that is small enough to fit in a purse or a pocket, yet it has all the rules you need to know about English grammar. It does not have assignments or exercises in it, but it does have all the rules and gives examples for each one. It is also fairly inexpensive.

Check the appendices of this book for some of the more common mistakes students make in papers and for some simple rules that will help fix them.

Learning Activity

Read your paper two more times. The first time, read it from start to finish, checking each word for spelling and for appropriateness (is it the exact word you want in that particular place?). The second time, read one sentence at a time, starting from the end of the paper and moving backwards. Use this reading to spot fragments, run-on sentences, and any mistakes that you know you make (if you know you have trouble with subject/verb agreement, make sure you read for that this time through).

Congratulations! You now know how to write an effective essay.

NOTES:

Appendix A: Top 10 Mistakes

1. FRAGMENTS

2. RUN-ONS

3. COMMA SPLICES

4. SPELLING

5. PRONOUN PROBLEMS

6. POINT OF VIEW SHIFTS

7. TENSE SHIFTS

8. SUBJECT-VERB AGREEMENT

9. INTRODUCTORY ELEMENTS

10. COMMONLY CONFUSED WORDS

Fragments

A sentence is usually a group of words that contains a subject, a verb, and (most of the time) an object (SVO). A group of words missing one of those elements is a fragment.

S   V   O
Billy took a test.
(S?) Took a test.
Billy (V?) a test.
Billy took (O?).

There are several common kinds of fragments:

1. No subject

I went to the mall. <u>Bought a coat.</u>

The underlined words are a fragment because they don't tell us *WHO* bought a coat. Even though we know that the "I" in the first sentence probably did the buying, there is no subject in the second group of words that tells us who did it, so it is a fragment.

2. Introductory elements improperly punctuated

A. Conditions

<u>If I get sick.</u> I will go home.

The "If" word creates a condition ("if I get sick"), which suggests that something will happen when that condition is true. "If I get sick" is not a complete sentence and needs a comma where the period is to join it to the next complete sentence, which tells what will happen if I get sick.

B. Prepositional phrases

<u>To be a doctor.</u> A student must study.

Something must happen in order for "someone" (who?) to be a doctor. That information has to be attached by using a comma instead of a period.

C. "-ing" or "-ed" words

<u>Waiting for the bus.</u> I got soaked.

Someone was waiting for the bus, but that information is not in this group of words. It is in the following sentence. Join the fragment to the following sentence with a comma instead of separating it with a period.

NOTE: In the above examples of introductory elements, a quick check is to place these fragments at the end of the following sentence. If they make sense there (A student must study to be a doctor.), then they need a comma when placed BEFORE that sentence.

There's a reason for this. In general, people like to get the important information up front, then the details or less important information. If your mother were in a wreck, you would not want me to come in and tell all the info about how the wreck happened before I told you your mother was involved. You'd much rather I told you the important information first (Your mother was in a wreck.) After you determine that your mother is okay, THEN you might be interested in hearing about the details of the wreck.

Combined sentences work the same way. The condition is the less important. We don't need a comma if we put that "less important" information after the "important" information. If we put it at the beginning, we separate it with a comma so the reader knows we've reversed that order.

Run-Ons

Two complete sentences that are not separated correctly or combined correctly make a run-on:

I went to the mall I bought a coat.

Each of the underlined groups of words above is a sentence. Each contains a subject, verb, and object. However, they are run together without any separating punctuation or without being properly joined. There are several ways to fix this (many of them from Dr. Wright Gooder's Comma Rules):

1. Separate into two sentences with a period.

I went to the mall. I bought a coat.

Now each of these groups of words has its own period, making each one a complete sentence. (Cs. Cs.)

2. Combine using a semi-colon.

I went to the mall; I bought a coat.

3. Combine using a comma and an "AND" word.

I went to the mall, and I bought a coat

4. Combine using an "IF" word in the middle and **NO COMMA**.

I went to the mall when I bought a coat

5. Combine using an "IF" word at the beginning and a comma following the "IF" group of words.

When I went to the mall, I bought a coat

Comma Splices

A comma splice is exactly the same thing as a run-on except that the writer put a comma where the period should be:

<u>I went to the mall,</u> <u>I bought a coat.</u>

Each of the underlined groups of words above is a sentence. Each contains a subject, verb, and object. A comma by itself is not enough of a punctuation mark to separate these two complete sentences. The ways to fix this mistake are the same as for a run-on:

1. Separate into two sentences with a period.

   <u>I went to the mall.</u> <u>I bought a coat.</u>

Now each of these groups of words has its own period, making each one a complete sentence. (Cs. Cs.)

2. Combine using a semi-colon.

   <u>I went to the mall;</u> <u>I bought a coat.</u>

3. Combine using a comma and an "AND" word.

   <u>I went to the mall,</u> and <u>I bought a coat</u>

4. Combine using an "IF" word in the middle and **NO COMMA**.

   <u>I went to the mall when</u> <u>I bought a coat</u>

5. Combine using an "IF" word at the beginning and a comma following the "IF" group of words.

   <u>When I went to the mall,</u> <u>I bought a coat.</u>

Spelling

Spelling is one of the hardest mistakes to solve. Many misspellings come from words that are commonly confused with each other (See Commonly Confused Words on page 72).

Here are two things that may help you improve your spelling:

1. 300 Most Common Words in English

Look up on the Internet "300 Most Common Words in English" or "300 Most Commonly Used Words in English."

Read through the list. These are the BASIC words that hold together all the other words in English. These 300 words make up (depending on which source you use) 65-70% of ALL WRITTEN ENGLISH.

Two-thirds or more of all the words you will ever read in English are in this list. Note how few "sophisticated" or hard words are on this list. I am not a fan of vocabulary lists in general but I am going to say that, if there were ever a list of words you need to know by heart, these 300 are them. Many of them will be in the Commonly Confused Words list as well ("there" and "their" for example). KNOW HOW TO SPELL THESE WORDS AND KNOW WHICH SPELLING MEANS WHAT.

2. YOUR vocabulary list

You need to keep a list of words that YOU misspell. I could give you a list of the 500 most commonly misspelled words, but that does not mean you use any of the words on that list. You need a list of words YOU spell incorrectly all the time. Here's how you do that:

Any time you get a paper, letter, report, note to your mother, etc. back and someone has indicated you spelled a word incorrectly, put that word on a list. Keep a small memo pad or something on you at all times if you can. Write the word down on that pad.

When you get a few words (once a week or so, probably), take each of those words and look it up in a dictionary, on Wikipedia, on a search engine. I don't care where or how you find out the correct spelling, but find it. Check it with another source to make sure it's correct. Also, read the definition in the dictionary for that spelling to be SURE it is the spelling that goes with the meaning you want. Then, do the following:

On a sheet of paper, make three columns—one for the wrong spelling, one of the correct spelling, and one for a hint to help you spell the word correctly. See the figure on the next page for an example.

Wrong spelling	Correct Spelling	Hint or Tip
buetiful	beautiful	be a utiful

Then, using the hint or tip that you came up with, S-L-O-W-L-Y use that tip to write the word 10 times in the center column. Two things: 1) Speed is not important here; don't rush through it, and 2) Don't cheat by writing 10 "b" letters, then 10 "e" letters, then 10 "a" letters, etc. The emphasis is on ingraining that hint or tip into your brain where it will live forever (we hope). It should, when finished, look something like this:

Wrong spelling	Correct Spelling	Hint or Tip
buetiful	beautiful	be a utiful
	beautiful	
	beautiful	
	beautiful	
	beautiful	
	beautiful	
	beautiful	
	beautiful	
	beautiful	
	beautiful	
	beautiful	

Then go on to the next word on your list:

Wrong spelling	Correct Spelling	Hint or Tip
buetiful	beautiful	be a utiful
	beautiful	
	beautiful	
	beautiful	
	beautiful	
	beautiful	
	beautiful	
	beautiful	
	beautiful	
	beautiful	
	beautiful	
Wensday	Wednesday	Wed nes day

Do this for every word on your list. If you continue to misspell a word after doing this 10 times, do it for 20 times the next week, then 30. If you get that far and you're still misspelling it, you might want to take a look at your hint or tip and change it.

The big advantage of this system is that you will be working with the words YOU use, not ones some scholar came up with that you don't ever use. Knowing how to spell "nomenclature" is great for a vocabulary test, but if you use "name" instead, that is the word you need to be spelling correctly. You will also be surprised to find that your vocabulary WILL increase as you use the dictionary because you will be exposed to new, interesting words for things.

Pronoun Problems

One of the most apparent mistakes on beginning writers' papers tends to be mistakes in using pronouns. Let's take a look at several of the areas where pronoun mistakes occur.

Pronoun-antecedent agreement

The rule says that pronouns have to agree with their antecedent in number, person, and gender.

We have to first know that a pronoun is a word that replaces a noun that has already been mentioned. So we don't have to say, "Bill wants to know if Bill can go to the mall," we usually say:

> *Bill wants to know if **he** can go to the mall.*

The pronoun "he" in this sentence refers back to "Bill." "Bill" is the antecedent (the thing that comes before the pronoun). That's all antecedent means. So, the pronoun "he" must match with the antecedent noun "Bill" in three ways.

1. Number—By number, we mean either singular (one) or plural (more than one). Bill is only one person, so Bill is singular. The pronoun we use later in the sentence (or in the next sentence or later) must also be singular. Our choices for a pronoun to replace "Bill" are "he" or "they." The word "they" means more than one person, so it would be plural. That doesn't match, number-wise, with "Bill." So, we use "he" because it refers to only one person:

> ~~"Bill" = 1; "they" => 1.~~

> "Bill" = 1; "he" = 1.

2. Person—There are three "persons" in regard to writing: first person (1st), second person (2nd), and third person (3rd). How's that for original naming? Let's get these straight.

1st = I, me. This is the person speaking. If I am writing this, I refer to the writer as "I" or "me" when I write. In our example above, "Bill" is not the person writing the sentence. We know this because he doesn't refer to himself as "I" or "me" when he writes. (The "I" is when the writer is the subject of the sentence—the on doing the action—and the "me" is when the writer is one having the action done to them.)

2nd = you, you. This is the person being spoken to. This is referring to the reader in a written work. Since the writer is writing to the reader about someone in the

instructions are often in second person, using the "understood YOU" instead of actually saying "you" in the sentence. "Choose three large ripe tomatoes" is the writer telling the reader to do that task –"(You) choose three large ripe tomatoes."

3rd—he, she, it; him, her, it; they, them. This is when the writer is talking to the reader ABOUT a third person. In our example above, Bill is not the writer or the reader; he is a third person separate from them that they are talking about. So, the writer refers to Bill as "he" later in the sentence.

 3. Gender. In English grammar, gender is either male, female, or neuter (neutral). Usually, the male and female roles do not give us trouble. We know if the subject we're talking about is one or the other. We know (or are at least reasonably sure) that Bill is a male. Therefore, pronouns referring to Bill will be either "he" or "him" and not "she" or "her." Pretty easy, right?

Where we do get into trouble is when we don't know the gender of the subject we're talking about. For example, if I say, "I am moving to Chicago and need to find a doctor there," neither you (the reader) nor I (the writer) have any idea whether the doctor I find there will be a male or a female, so we are in a dilemma. Since we don't know the gender, the pronoun should be neuter (it), but LONG, LONG AGO people decided that it wasn't nice to call other people "it." Logical, maybe, but not nice. Grammatically, that is exactly what we should do here, but we don't.

Since it isn't nice to call people "it," the rule for hundreds of years was to refer to a "neuter" person as "he or him," the masculine pronouns. That came under fire when society decided that was gender biased. So, we're stuck. What do we do?

An easy way is to use plurals. If you can change both the antecedent and the pronoun to plurals, you're okay, like "I am moving to Chicago and need to find doctors there. I hope I find some with their offices near my work." That's fine if I need more than one doctor, but if I am only looking for one doctor, it doesn't work.

Another way is to write around it. We could not refer to gender at all and say something like, "I am moving to Chicago and need to find doctors there. I hope I find one with *an office* near my work."

We could say, "I am moving to Chicago and to find a doctor there. I hope I find one with *his or her* office near my work." That works fine for one or two sentences, but gets monotonous and irritating in a longer work. Others proclaim alternating "him" or "he" in one paragraph and "her" or "she" in another, but that is confusing to the reader. And our main goal in writing is to NOT CONFUSE the reader, so I'm not partial to that one either.

Your best bet is to write around it or to make the antecedent and pronoun plural. Each instructor has a preference; be sure to ask in each course.

Point of View Shifts

Point of View shifts (POV) occur when you are writing a sentence in one of the "persons" we talked about in the pronouns section—first person, second person, or third person—and you move from one to the other for no reason.

The most common mistake is when a person is writing in third person (he, she, it) and shifts to second person (you, you):

College students must learn to overcome many problems when you go to college.

The POV of the first part of the sentence is third person (College students = they, them), but the POV of the second part is in second person (you). The problem is that the "you" of the second part of the sentence is made up of the same people as in the first part, "college students." To correct it, the writer must change the POV of the second part of the sentence.

*College students must learn to overcome many problems when **they** go to college.*

Writers often shift back and forth between third person and second person because, in casual conversation, they use these words interchangeably. "You" in casual conversation can mean mankind or people in general. Because of this, many people think of "you" as third person for "they" or "them," but that is not what it means. In writing, it usually means the person reading what is written.

Here's a common passage with point of view problems:

Football players often suffer life-altering injuries. They can blow their knee out when you get hit by a linebacker helmet to the knee or catch your foot in the grass as a tackler hits you. Some positions are more vulnerable than others. You don't shatter your knee as often as a place kicker or punter. Linemen, running backs, and receivers will often have knee injuries that put you out of the game, maybe for a season, maybe for life.

Here's that passage corrected for POV problems:

*Football players often suffer life-altering injuries. They can blow their knee out when ~~you~~ **they** get hit by a linebacker helmet to the knee or catch ~~your~~ **their** foot in the grass as a tackler hits ~~you~~ **them**. Some positions are more vulnerable than others. ~~You~~ **They** don't shatter ~~your~~ **their** knee as often as a place kicker or punter. Linemen, running backs, and receivers will often have knee injuries that put ~~you~~ **them** out of the game, maybe for a season, maybe for life.*

Verb Tense Shifts

Shifts in verb tense occur when a person writes about things that all happened in a particular tense (time)—past, present, or future, but shifts back and forth between the tenses.

Let's say that you're talking about your experience in the high school band in an essay for your college writing class. Since you are now in college, all the high school events happened in your past. So, you want to write the essay in past tense:

> *High school band was a pleasant experience for me. I met many interesting people, learned to play the trombone, and realized how much music meant to me. One of the people I met in my high school band was Leonard Trabowski, the drum major. I am walking down the hall when I bump into him coming out of the band director's office. The impact knocked me to the floor, and he immediately stopped to help me up. He picks up my books and hands them to me.*

Notice that many of the verbs used are in past tense, many of them ending in "ed." However, even though ALL of these events happened in the past, this writer has used present tense for some of the verbs. Present tense means the action is happening now or is an ongoing action. Every time the writer moves from past to present or present to past is a verb tense. Here's the same passage with the verb tense problem corrected:

> *High school band was a pleasant experience for me. I met many interesting people, learned to play the trombone, and realized how much music meant to me. One of the people I met in my high school band was Leonard Trabowski, the drum major. I ~~am~~ **was** walking down the hall when I ~~bump~~ **bumped** into him coming out of the band director's office. The impact knocked me to the floor, and he immediately stopped to help me up. He ~~picks~~ **picked** up my books and ~~hands~~ **handed** them to me.*

To catch this kind of mistake, try to ask yourself "When did this happen?" as you proofread each sentence. I (or you, he, she, it, we, they) did this in the past? I do this or am doing this now in the present? Or I will be doing this in the future?

Not all tense shifts are wrong. Tense shifts tell the reader WHEN something happened. So you could have a tense shift if the action moves in time:

> *My father started me fishing when I was only three years old. I spent every one of my next 10 birthdays on the lake with my dad, usually before the sun came up. We jigged for crappie from the docks, trolled for bass in the middle of the lake, and gobbed blood bait on treble hooks for catfish. Two months from now,*

it last week on the Internet. The day I turn 18, my dad and I will bait our hooks with chum on a deep-sea fishing boat off the coast of Key West.

There were several tense shifts in the above passage, but all of them are tense shifts "for a reason." The writer starts in past tense, describing all the birthdays she has spent fishing with her dad IN THE PAST. The reader gets a clue that there's a tense shift coming with the words "Two months from now," that tells us she is going to talk about something IN THE FUTURE. So, when she uses "will turn 18" instead of "turned 18," the reader is not confused as to when this happens. The very next sentence goes back to past tense—another tense shift—but for a reason; her father "told" her "last night" (PAST) that he "has" a special present.

WHOA! A tense shift in the middle of a sentence? Is that okay? Yes, because it is "for a reason"—he still has the present for her. In the final sentence, shifting to future tense is okay because that action will take place in the future. So, you can see that there are times for tense shifts, but you have to have a reason for them.

Another place you can shift tense is in an example:

I enjoy going to concerts. They make me feel like I am part of great music. I especially like new bands on the edge of the musical experience. For example, last weekend, I went to a tiny, dark, out-of-the-way club in Dallas and heard a band that had only played in its garage until that night. They were fantastic. They played some classic rock-and-roll but also performed some of their new techno-classical-country-hip hop songs as well. I left the club with a sense of discovery. I like to hear new bands that push the edge of the musical envelope. I also play in a band called the Misfit String Quartet. It is made up of two six-string guitars, a bass guitar, and a violin. We don't play in clubs yet, but someday, maybe we will.

Notice that the first part of the passage is in present tense—what this person enjoys doing now or on an ongoing basis. When he gets to the example, he shifts to past tense because the event in the example happened "last weekend." He stays in past tense because all the actions described happened during that weekend.

However, once he is finished with the example, the writer reverts back to present tense with "I like to hear new bands …" and stays in present tense until the end when he makes a prediction about the future. Often, student writers will stay in the same tense as the example even after they're describing events NOT in the example.

Subject-Verb Agreement

The subject of a sentence and the verb that acts with it have to agree in number. Generally, this rule is stated as "a singular subject takes a singular verb and a plural subject takes a plural verb."

Deciding whether a subject is singular or plural is fairly easy. Is the subject an "it" or a "they?" If the subject is an "it," then the subject is singular. If the subject is a "they," then the subject is plural.

Deciding whether a verb is singular or plural is not so easy, especially with a verb like the most common English one—"to be." Most of us know the following chart:

Singular	Plural
I am	We are
You are	You are
He, She, It is	They are

What is the plural verb? Very obviously, it seems to be "are." As long as the subject is more than one—"We," "You" (a group), "They"—the plural subject matches with the plural verb—"are."

But what is the singular verb in the above chart? HMMM! Not so easy, is it? If you use "I" the singular verb is "am" while the singular subjects "He," She," or "It" get the singular verb is. So, obviously, "am" and "is" are singular subjects.

What about "You" when it means only the reader, though? The "singular" verb used there is "are" which is … uh … plural, isn't it?

This is one of the problems we have with "singular" and "plural" verbs. The most used verb in English—"to be"—does not follow the rule, it seems. So, just learn which one goes with what in this verb form.

With few exceptions, though, we can give you a pretty good rule for how verbs work in English, and this is the one most of us know. Most of the problems in subject-verb agreement are in the present tense. Most of them happen in the third person singular (he, she, it) and plural (they) forms. Here's the basic rule:

Use the "to _____" form of the verb—"to run," for example—for all but the third person singular form.

I run	We run
You run	You run
He, She, It _____	They run

For the third person singular, add an "s" to the "to _____" form:

I run	We run
You run	You run
He, She, It <u>runs</u>	They run

Most of us learn this rule pretty early on. Then we apply it to all the verbs we know. If we apply it to ALL of them, then we get this common form in some dialects:

I be	We be
You be	You be
He, She, It <u>bes</u>	They be

While this form is incorrect, the speaker is actually applying the basic rule they've learned. They just now have to learn that the most used verb in the English language is, in fact, the biggest exception to that rule.

The biggest place subject-verb agreement errors occur is when there are extra words between the subject and the verb. Prepositional phrases describing the subject are one of the biggest causes of subject-verb disagreement.

Few of us would ever say, "The boy go home every day after school." Most of us would say, "The boy goes home every day after school." However, if we say, "The boy who stops to smell the roses …" then we can get confused. Do we say "go" or "goes" in this case?

The reason is that the subject and verb are now apart, not side by side like we usually think of them. Our ear hears "roses" before the verb and we try to make "go" fit as the verb. However, it is not the roses that are on their way home; it is the boy. So we need to disregard the words in between the subject and the verb and match them as if those words weren't there. We end up with "The boy who stops to smell the roses goes home every day after school," even though "roses grows" just doesn't sound right.

To determine if it is or is not right, we just have to disregard the words in between:

"The boy ~~who stops to smell the roses~~ goes home every day after school."

Do that and you will get it right almost every time.

Introductory Elements

There are many types of introductory elements that are written BEFORE the main part of the sentence. Many of these have to be separated from the main part of the sentence with a comma. Here is a list of some of the most common ones with explanations following:

- "If" clauses

- Prepositional phrases

- -ing and –ed clauses

- Transitions

"If" clauses

Remember the "if" clauses from the Comma Rules section? When they appear at the beginning of the sentence, they need to be separated from the rest of the sentence with a comma:

"If I go to the mall, I will buy something."

By having the "if" word attached to it, the complete sentence (independent clause) becomes "not a complete sentence" (dependent clause). In general, people like to get the important information up front, then the details (check out the Unity section, especially the part about general to specific). If we change that order, we do something to help the reader realize that.

Had we said, "I will buy something if I go to the mall," then the main part of the sentence comes first and the details (the condition of when that will happen) comes at the end. So, because we like to get info this way, we don't need a comma here.

HOWEVER, if we switch this order and put the less important info up front, we need a comma AFTER the complete clause. One way to watch for this structure is to look for any "if" words at the beginning of a sentence. The most commonly used ones are "if," "because," "when," and "since." For a more complete list, do an Internet search for "subordinating conjunctions." When you see one of these words at the beginning of a sentence, ask yourself what the "if" is (or the "when" or "since" etc.). At the END of the "if" clause, place a comma. Make sure you have ALL of the "if" clause before you put the comma in, though:

"If I go home to see my mother for Christmas, I will take her the present I bought her."

The "if" clause is not "If I go home." That's not all of it. It's not "If I go home to see my mother." That's not all of it. The complete "if" clause is "If I go home to see my mother for Christmas." So, you need the comma after "Christmas."

Prepositional phrases

Prepositions are all those little words that connect things together. Below are a few examples:

to

for

with

on

near

by

under

over

beside

from

They are used to connect a noun with another part of the sentence. The underlined part of the following sentences below are prepositional phrases:

"I have a house <u>in the city</u>."

When we discussed order of importance, we talked about how people like the most important information up front and the details to follow. In the sentence above, "I have a house" is information you need to know in order for "in the city" (where that house is) to make sense. So, we often say it or write just like the sentence above.

However, we can put the "less important" information first as long as we clue the reader that we're doing it. So, if I take "in the city" and put it at the beginning of the sentence, that's okay, but I have to separate it with a comma from the rest of the sentence so the reader knows what's going on:

"In the city, I have a house."

The comma lets the reader know that "In the city" is not a complete sentence; it is attached to the complete sentence that follows. Here are a few more examples:

"I can get there easily from your house."

"From your house, I can get there easily."

"A student must study very hard to be a doctor or a lawyer."

"To be a doctor or a lawyer, a student must study very hard."

"I want to decorate the house in blue and white for the Christmas party."

"For the Christmas party, I want to decorate the house in blue and white."

-ing and –ed clauses

Clauses starting with "-ing" and "-ed" words usually begin with a verb, such as, "waiting for my mother" or "arrested by the police." They usually do not have a subject included, which makes them dependent clauses that cannot stand by themselves as a separate sentence. Because of that, they fall into that category of "less important" information in the sentence. They are the details we normally put AFTER the important information. Again, if we move that information to the front, we need to separate it by commas. Here are a couple of examples:

"I sat in the mall parking lot for three hours waiting for my mother."

"Waiting for my mother, I sat in the mall parking lot for three hours."

"The drug dealer ratted on his buddies when he was arrested by police."

"Arrested by police, the drug dealer ratted on his buddies."

Notice that, in the drug dealer sentence, the clause "arrested by police" didn't fit by itself at the end of the sentence. It needed "when he" to explain that it was not the buddies who were arrested. We could have brought that whole clause to the front ("If" clause rule), but we decided to go with only "arrested by police." This brings up an interesting rule—dangling modifiers.

These "-ing" and "-ed" clauses can often be dangling modifiers, which means they are not referring to the correct noun in the sentence. When placed at the front of a sentence, "-ing" and "-ed" clauses must refer to the subject of the sentence—the one that follows the comma:

"Smoking a cigar, my lab lay beside my chair as I read the evening paper."

If the "-ing" clause has to refer to the subject that follows the comma, then this writer just told us that his lab smokes cigars. That is probably not what he meant. You would have to rewrite the sentence to put the correct subject after the comma:

"Smoking a cigar, I read the evening paper as my lab lay beside my chair."

Transitions

There are many transitions at the beginning of sentences. Many of these were discussed in the Unity section. Transitions tell a reader how the sentence they just finished reading is connected to the next sentence. Before they even read the next sentence, the reader can form an educated guess as to what that sentence will be about.

"John is a very good student. However, …"

The "however" lets the reader know that the next sentence is probably going to be something bad about John, an opposite from the good information about him in the first sentence.

"John is a very good student. However, he is a very bad athlete."

Other kinds of transitions lead the reader to a different idea of what the next sentence will be about.

"John is a very good student. Therefore, …"

This lets the reader know that, whatever the next sentence says, it will be about something that comes from John being a good student, something that was caused by his being a good student.

"John is a very good student. Therefore, he is getting a full scholarship to Princeton."

Commonly Confused Words

Most writers have words that are hard for them to spell or that they get confused with other words. Here are some that are absolute basics for you to know for college writing. You can ask your instructor, use a dictionary, use a grammar book, do an Internet search, or work with a study group to figure out when to use which of the following words. This should be an interactive effort on your part. I would do this much like the way I suggested doing your spelling words.

A, An, And

Accept, Except

Advice, Advise

A Lot, Allot (not A lot)

Are, Our

Breath, Breathe

Choose, Chose, Chosen

Clothes, Cloths

Every Day, Everyday

Fewer, Less

Have, Of

Its, It's

Lay, Lie

Lead, Led

Loose, Lose

Passed, Past

Personal, Personnel

Quiet, Quit, Quite

Raise, Rise

Role, Roll

Set, Sit

Than, Then

Their, There, They're

To, Too

Waist, Waste

Were, We're, Where

Whose, Who's

Your, You're

NOTES:

Appendix B: Revision Checklist

Peer Reviewer's Name:_____

Writer's Name:_____

Editing Checklist	Yes/No?	Where
Is there a clear thesis? Do you know up front what the paper is about? Is the main idea clear?		
Comments:		
Are the major points of the main idea clear to the reader BEFORE the writer goes into detail about them?		
Comments:		
Are the main points supported (proven) by the details?		
Comments:		
Are there SUFFICIENT details to prove (or support) the points?		
Comments:		
Are the details grouped with the main points they support?		
Comments:		
Are the details abstract or concrete ("somebody could cause problems" or "a disgruntled employee could report sexual harassment to a supervisor")?		
Comments:		
Are there specific examples used throughout the paper?		

Editing Checklist	Yes/No?	Where
Comments:		
Were all words spelled correctly?		
Comments:		
Did the writer use capital letters: at the beginning of a sentence?		
for proper nouns [names]?		
Comments:		
Did they correctly: use periods?		
use commas?		
use question marks?		
used the right tenses, eg. did/done?		
Comments:		
Does it make sense?		
Comments:		
Is it interesting?		
Comments:		
When finished, was there something else you still wanted to know about the subject?		
Comments:		
Are there any other comments you think would be beneficial to this student for improving this paper?		

Appendix C: The Revision Process in Action

Example Draft #1

Dear John:

I want a man who knows what love is all about you are generous kind thoughtful people who are not like you admit to being useless and inferior you have ruined me for other men I yearn for you I have no feelings whatsoever when we're apart I can be forever happy will you let me be yours

Jane

Example Draft #2

Dear John:

I want a man who knows what love is. All about you are generous, kind, thoughtful people, who are not like you. Admit to being useless and inferior. You have ruined me. For other men, I yearn. For you, I have no feelings whatsoever. When we're apart, I can be forever happy.

Will you let me be?

Yours,

Jane

Example Draft #3

Dear John:

I want a man who knows what love is all about. You are generous, kind, thoughtful. People who are not like you admit to being useless and inferior. You have ruined me for other men. I yearn for you. I have no feelings whatsoever when we're apart. I can be forever happy. Will you let me be yours?

Jane

NOTES:

Appendix D: Wilhite's Comma Rules

<u>Rule #1</u>

1, 2, and 3

Items in a series

I like dogs, cats, and horses.

<u>Rule #2</u>

Cs, and cs.

Two complete sentences joined by any "and" list word: and, but, or, yet, so, for.

Joe was late for class, and he was not allowed to take the test.

<u>Rule #3</u>

Cs if cs.

Two complete sentences joined by an "if" list word (subordinate conjunctions list): if, because, when, since.

Joe will not be allowed to take the test if he is late for class.
Joe was not allowed to take the test because he was late for class.

<u>Rule #4</u>

If cs, cs.

If an "if" list word (see above) starts a sentence, it is separated from the main part of the sentence with a comma.

If Joe is late for class, he will not be allowed to take the test.
Because Joe was late for class, he was not allowed to take the test.

<u>Rule #5</u>

C, if cs, s.

If an element (word, phrase, or clause) interrupts the flow of the main sentence, it must be separated on both ends with commas.

Joe will not be allowed, if he is late for class, to take the test.

NOTES:

Appendix E: Essay Organization Template

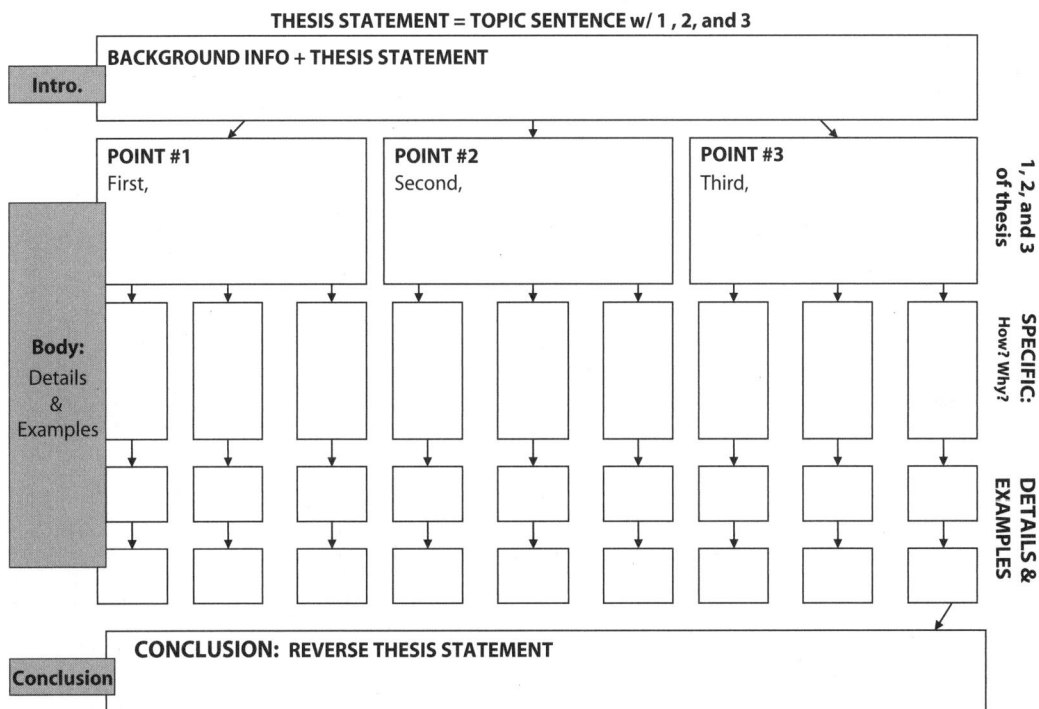

This appendix shows you how all the paragraph templates fit into the overall organization of your essay.

The first diagram—the essay organization template—has the introduction paragraph as the box at the top, then smaller templates (but with the same information as the larger ones you've done) as the body in the middle. Finally, it also shows a long box at the bottom as the conclusion.

The diagrams after that have a stand-alone template for each of the paragraphs shown in the overall essay organization template.

Essay Organization Template

THESIS STATEMENT = TOPIC SENTENCE w/ 1 , 2, and 3

Intro.	**BACKGROUND INFO + THESIS STATEMENT**

| **POINT #1** First, | **POINT #2** Second, | **POINT #3** Third, | 1, 2, and 3 of thesis |

Body: Details & Examples — SPECIFIC: How? Why? — DETAILS & EXAMPLES

Conclusion	**CONCLUSION:** REVERSE THESIS STATEMENT

Paragraph Organization Template

Now, let's look at a full-page template for each paragraph you will write for an essay.

Introduction Paragraph

General Statement

↓

Thesis Statement

Body Paragraphs (Points 1-3)

SPECIFIC: How? Why?

DETAILS & EXAMPLES

Point #1

First,

→ →

→ →

→ →

SPECIFIC:
How? Why?

DETAILS & EXAMPLES

Point #2
Second,

SPECIFIC: How? Why?   DETAILS & EXAMPLES

Point #3

Third,

Conclusion Paragraph

Reverse Your Thesis Statement: "Because 1, 2, and 3, ..."

Conclusion

Index

About the Author

George Wilhite is the chair of the English department at Texas State Technical College in Waco whose specialty has been developmental writing for nearly fifteen years. He also teaches developmental English classes at Baylor University and was the founder of the Waco Writers Workshop at McLennan Community College.

Wilhite has been a professional, published writer for nearly thirty years. He was a journalist—writer, editor, publisher—for twenty-plus years, including work in newspapers, magazines, public relations, and advertising. He has garnered awards from the National Newspaper Association, Texas Press Association, and South Texas Press Association, as well as an ADDY award for advertising.

A published novelist and short story writer, his published fiction includes short stories which have appeared in anthologies, magazines, and literary magazines. His first novel, *The Texas Rodeo Murder*, is available from Eakin Press or from the author at www.drwrightgooder.webs.com.

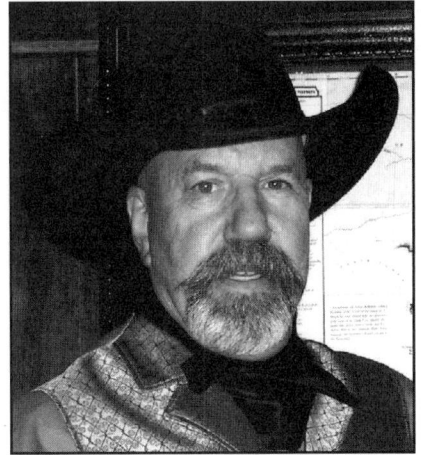

About TSTC Publishing

Established in 2004, TSTC Publishing is a provider of high-end technical instructional materials and related information to institutions of higher education and private industry. "High end" refers simultaneously to the information delivered, the various delivery formats of that information, and the marketing of materials produced. More information about the products and services offered by TSTC Publishing may be found at its Web site: http://publishing.tstc.edu/.

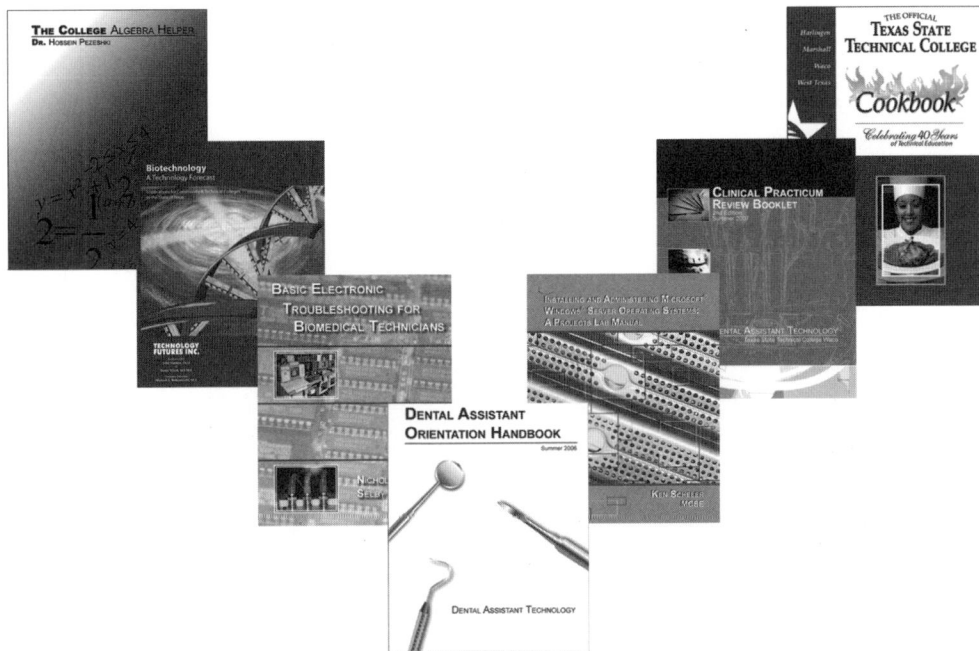